# THE TRUTH ABOUT EARLY AMERICAN HISTORY

# THE TRUTH ABOUT U.S. SYMBOLS

CHARLOTTE TAYLOR

Please visit our website, www.enslow.com. For a free color catalog of all our high-quality books, call toll free 1-800-398-2504 or fax 1-877-980-4454.

**Cataloging-in-Publication Data**
Names: Taylor, Charlotte, 1978-.
Title: The truth about U.S. symbols / Charlotte Taylor.
Description: New York : Enslow Publishing, 2023. | Series: The truth about early American history | Includes glossary and index.
Identifiers: ISBN 9781978527980 (pbk.) | ISBN 9781978528000 (library bound) | ISBN 9781978527997 (6pack) | ISBN 9781978528017 (ebook)
Subjects: LCSH: Emblems, National–United States–Juvenile literature. | Signs and symbols–United States–Juvenile literature. | National monuments–United States–Juvenile literature.
Classification: LCC JC346.T39 2023 | DDC 929.90973–dc23

Published in 2023 by
**Enslow Publishing**
29 E. 21st Street
New York, NY 10010

Portions of this work were originally authored by Jill Keppeler and published as *Betsy Ross Didn't Create the American Flag: Exposing Myths About U.S. Symbols*. All new material in this edition was authored by Charlotte Taylor.

Designer: Rachel Rising
Editor: Megan Quick

Photo credits: Cover, IanDagnall Computing / Alamy Stock Photo; Cover, pp. 1-6, 8, 10-12, 14, 16, 18, 20, 22-26, 28, 30-32 pashabo/Shutterstock.com; Cover, pp. 1-6, 8, 10-12, 14, 16, 18, 20, 22-26, 28, 30-32 orangeberry/Shutterstock.com; Cover, pp. 1-6, 8, 10-12, 14, 16, 18, 20, 22-26, 28, 30-32 iulias/Shutterstock.com; Cover, Brian A Jackson/Shutterstock.com; Cover, pp. 1, 3, 5, 6, 8,11, 12, 14, 16, 18, 20, 23, 25, 28, 30-32 Epifantsev/Shutterstock.com; p. 4 Christian Delbert/Shutterstock.com; p. 5 Leena Robinson/Shutterstock.com; p. 7 https://commons.wikimedia.org/wiki/File:Thirteencolonies_politics_cropped.jpg; p. 9 Science History Images / Alamy Stock Photo; p. 10 Songquan Deng/Shutterstock.com; p. 11 trekandshoot/Shutterstock.com; p. 13 https://en.wikipedia.org/wiki/File:Arrival_of_Liberty_Bell_in_Allentown_-_1777.jpg; p. 15 https://commons.wikimedia.org/wiki/File:Great_Seal_of_the_United_States_(obverse).svg; pp. 15, 19 s_oleg/Shutterstock.com; p. 17 FloridaStock/Shutterstock.com; p. 19 https://commons.wikimedia.org/wiki/File:J._M._Flagg,_I_Want_You_for_U.S._Army_poster_(1917).jpg; p. 21 https://commons.wikimedia.org/wiki/File:Putting_his_foot_down.jpg; p. 22 https://commons.wikimedia.org/wiki/File:The_President%27s_House_by_George_Munger,_1814-1815_-_Crop.jpg; p. 23 Sagittarius Pro/Shutterstock.com; p. 24 Pigprox/Shutterstock.com; p. 25 https://en.wikipedia.org/wiki/File:Washington-Monument-1885.png; p. 27 Checubus/Shutterstock.com; p. 29 Rawpixel.com/Shutterstock.com.

Printed in the United States of America

Some of the images in this book illustrate individuals who are models. The depictions do not imply actual situations or events.

CPSIA compliance information: Batch #CSENS23: For further information contact Enslow Publishing, New York, New York, at 1-800-398-2504.

Find us on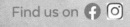

# CONTENTS

WORDS IN THE GLOSSARY APPEAR IN **BOLD** TYPE
THE FIRST TIME THEY ARE USED IN THE TEXT.

# IMAGES OF AMERICA

There are many **symbols** of the United States. They can be flags, colors, or animals that stand for the country and its history. Each symbol has a story behind it. You have probably heard some of these stories. But are they all true?

The U.S. flag has many nicknames, including "Old Glory" and "the Stars and Stripes."

Sometimes, stories that are passed down over the years are not true. The facts might get mixed up or forgotten. Did Betsy Ross make the first American flag? Was the national bird supposed to be a turkey? Let's find out the truth about U.S. symbols.

BETSY ROSS FLAG

## EXPLORE MORE!

THE AMERICAN FLAG IS AN IMPORTANT U.S. SYMBOL THAT SHOULD BE TREATED CAREFULLY. THERE IS A COMMON BELIEF THAT IF A U.S. FLAG TOUCHES THE GROUND, IT MUST BE DESTROYED. THIS IS NOT TRUE. THE FLAG SHOULD NOT TOUCH THE GROUND, BUT IF IT DOES, IT CAN BE CLEANED AND USED AGAIN.

# WHO MADE THE FLAG?

The **design** for the first official American flag was authorized on June 14, 1777. It had 13 red and white stripes, as well as 13 white stars on a field of blue. Who created this design? Many people say it was Betsy Ross. But others claim that's not true.

At the time, the 13 British colonies were fighting a war to break free from British rule. George Washington, who would become the first U.S. president, wanted a flag to **represent** the new country. The story says he visited Ross at her shop in Philadelphia, Pennsylvania, and asked her to sew the flag. She agreed. But did this really happen?

## EXPLORE MORE!

BETSY ROSS TOLD PEOPLE THAT GEORGE WASHINGTON AND TWO OTHER MEN CAME TO HER WITH A DESIGN FOR THE FLAG. SHE SAID SHE LOOKED AT IT AND SUGGESTED CHANGING THE NUMBER OF POINTS ON THE STARS FROM SIX TO FIVE.

Fort Michilimackinac

Montreal

Huron

Sankt-Lorenz-Strom

Fort Frontenac

Ontario

Fort Niagara

Fort Detroit

Erie

**(VERMONT)**

Connecticut

**MAINE** (ZU MASS.)

**NEW HAMPSHIRE**

Portsmouth

**NEW YORK**

**MASS.**

Salem

Boston

**PLYMOUTH** (1620-98)

Hudson

**CONN.**

Hartford

Providence

Newport

**NEW HAVEN** (1638-48)

**RHODE ISLAND**

Fort Duquesne

**PENN-SYLVANIA**

Ohio

New York

Burlington

Philadelphia

New Castle

**NEW JERSEY**

Baltimore

Potomac

**DELAWARE**

**MARYLAND**

**THE ORIGINAL 13 COLONIES**

**VIRGINIA**

Williamsburg

✘ Jamestown (1608)

✘ Ranaoke Island (1586–88)

**NORTH CAROLINA**

New Bern

**SOUTH CAROLINA**

The U.S. flag's 13 stripes stand for the original 13 colonies, while each star stands for a state.

Charleston

**GEORGIA**

Savannah

St. Augustine

There are several problems with the Betsy Ross tale. First, it did not become public until about 100 years later, when her grandson told some people the story. Second, there is no **proof** that the meeting with Washington ever took place.

Today, most **historians** agree that Ross probably did not make the first flag. Many believe that Francis Hopkinson, a signer of the **Declaration of Independence**, came up with the design. In fact, he asked the government to pay him for the work. He was turned down because others worked on the design as well.

## EXPLORE MORE!

MANY PEOPLE DOUBT THE STORY OF GEORGE WASHINGTON VISITING BETSY ROSS'S SHOP IN PHILADELPHIA. BUT IT IS LIKELY THE TWO HAD MET BEFORE. ROSS ATTENDED THE SAME CHURCH AS WASHINGTON AND OTHER IMPORTANT FIGURES. THERE ARE ALSO REPORTS THAT WASHINGTON BOUGHT BED CURTAINS FROM ROSS IN 1774.

Despite a lack of proof, the story of Betsy Ross making the first U.S. flag has been passed along and even taught in schools.

# LET FREEDOM RING

The Liberty Bell has long been a symbol of freedom in America. Today, the bell stands in Philadelphia, across from the building where the official Declaration of Independence was approved on July 4, 1776. Many people believe the bell got its famous crack on that date. But the truth is that the bell did not even ring that day!

The Liberty Bell sits across the street from Independence Hall, which was first known as the Pennsylvania State House.

In Philadelphia, the Declaration of Independence was not read in public for the first time until July 8, 1776. This means that there were no celebrations of American freedom—and no bell ringing—on July 4. It is very unlikely that the crack formed then.

INDEPENDENCE HALL

## EXPLORE MORE!

IN 1776, THE LIBERTY BELL HUNG IN A TOWER IN THE PENNSYLVANIA STATE HOUSE. IT WAS ORIGINALLY CALLED THE STATE HOUSE BELL. ITS NAME WAS CHANGED TO THE LIBERTY BELL IN THE 1830s, WHEN IT BECAME A SYMBOL OF SUPPORT FOR THE ANTISLAVERY MOVEMENT.

So, how did the Liberty Bell get its crack? Nobody knows for sure. However, many historians believe that the bell simply rang so often that it started to break down. They think that the crack probably formed in the 1840s after many years of use.

Sometime after the famous crack appeared, another one weakened the bell even more. The bell has not rung since then. No one has heard the sound of the Liberty Bell since February 1846, when it rang in honor of George Washington's birthday.

## EXPLORE MORE!

THE LIBERTY BELL IS NOT RUNG ANYMORE, BUT IT IS STILL USED ON THE FOURTH OF JULY. EACH YEAR, CHILDREN WITH A FAMILY CONNECTION TO SIGNERS OF THE DECLARATION OF INDEPENDENCE GET TO TAP THE LIBERTY BELL.

During the American Revolution, the Liberty Bell was moved and hidden in a church to keep it out of British hands.

# FLYING HIGH

The bald eagle first became a national symbol of the United States on June 20, 1782. Government leaders picked the bird because it is a symbol of strength. Also, this eagle can only be found in North America.

The bald eagle's picture is part of the Great Seal of the United States. The **federal** government places the Great Seal on important **documents**. Benjamin Franklin was one of the men who worked on the design of the Great Seal. Some stories say Franklin argued that the wild turkey should be the symbol of the United States. This is a **myth**.

## EXPLORE MORE!

THE BALD EAGLE'S NAME MIGHT MAKE YOU THINK THAT ITS HEAD IS BARE. THIS ISN'T TRUE. THE BALD EAGLE HAS SHORT, SNOW-WHITE FEATHERS ON ITS HEAD. ITS BODY AND WINGS HAVE BROWN FEATHERS, WHILE ITS BEAK AND FEET ARE YELLOW.

E PLURIBUS UNUM

The bald eagle on the Great Seal holds arrows and an olive branch as symbols of war and peace.

It is true that Ben Franklin was not a fan of the bald eagle's **image** on the Great Seal. The picture looked more like a turkey, he told his daughter in 1784. He claimed that the bald eagle had "bad moral character" and said the bird was "too lazy to fish for himself."

Franklin went on to call the turkey more "respectable" and "a bird of courage." However, he did not complain to other leaders about the choice of the bald eagle as the national bird, as some stories say. And he never suggested that the turkey should be the official American bird.

## EXPLORE MORE!

BALD EAGLES ARE STRONG HUNTERS. THEY EAT SNAKES, SQUIRRELS, RABBITS, AND OTHER BIRDS. THEY EAT DEAD ANIMALS AS WELL. SOMETIMES THEY ATTACK OTHER BIRDS AND STEAL FISH FROM THEM. THIS IS PROBABLY WHY BEN FRANKLIN HAD A LOW OPINION OF THE BALD EAGLE.

Bald eagles almost died out in the mid-1900s. Today, their population has grown to more than 300,000.

# AMERICA'S UNCLE

Uncle Sam is a popular symbol of the United States. You have probably seen drawings of the man with a white beard, who is always dressed in red, white, and blue. But you might not know where this familiar figure came from.

Many people believe that the Uncle Sam character was made up in the early 1900s. During World War I (1914–1918) and World War II (1939–1945), his image appeared on **recruitment** posters with the words "I Want YOU for U.S. Army." This is the Uncle Sam that most people know. But he was around long before then.

## EXPLORE MORE!

JAMES MONTGOMERY FLAGG DREW THE PICTURE OF UNCLE SAM THAT WAS FIRST USED IN WORLD WAR I RECRUITING POSTERS. HE BORROWED THE DESIGN FROM A SIMILAR BRITISH POSTER. FLAGG USED HIS OWN FACE AS A MODEL FOR UNCLE SAM.

About 4 million copies of the Uncle Sam "I Want YOU" posters were printed during World War I.

The song "Yankee Doodle" sometimes includes the lines: "Uncle Sam came there to change/Some pancakes and some onions." The song was first printed in the 1750s. But the most well-known Uncle Sam tale got its start during the War of 1812.

A man named Samuel Wilson supplied meat to the American soldiers. The meat was sent in barrels marked with the letters "U.S." The story says soldiers started joking that the meat was from "Uncle Sam" Wilson. Many doubt this is true, though. There's no record of this story until 1842, years after the war.

## EXPLORE MORE!

AMERICAN CARTOONISTS DREW THE UNCLE SAM CHARACTER AS EARLY AS THE 1830s. THEN, IN THE 1870s, THOMAS NAST DREW HIM AS A SKINNY, BEARDED FIGURE DRESSED IN RED, WHITE, AND BLUE. NAST DID NOT CREATE UNCLE SAM AS SOME PEOPLE BELIEVE. BUT, HE DID MAKE HIM POPULAR.

In cartoons like this one from 1899, Uncle Sam represents the U.S. government.

TRADE TREATY WITH CHINA

MAP OF CHINA

21

# SYMBOLS OF THE CAPITAL

The White House in Washington, DC, became the home of the American president in 1800. But during the War of 1812, British troops set fire to the building. There is a myth that it was painted white to cover up the burn marks from the fire, and that coat of white paint is how it got its name. This is not true.

A painting shows the White House after the fire in 1814.

The White House had a white coloring from the time it was built. It was sometimes called the White House, but usually it was called the Executive Mansion or the President's House. It wasn't officially named the White House until President Theodore Roosevelt made it so in 1901.

## EXPLORE MORE!

JAMES MADISON WAS THE PRESIDENT IN 1814 WHEN THE BRITISH SET FIRE TO THE WHITE HOUSE. HE HAD ALREADY FLED WHEN THE BRITISH TROOPS ARRIVED. MADISON WAS NO LONGER PRESIDENT BY THE TIME THE WHITE HOUSE WAS READY TO BE LIVED IN AGAIN, IN 1817.

The Washington Monument in Washington, DC, is very easy to spot. It is the tallest structure in the city. This famous monument was built in honor of George Washington.

The Washington Monument stands at one end of the National Mall, seen here. Notice the change in the color of the stone in the monument.

The Washington Monument is made of stone. About a third of the way up, the stone changes color. Some people think this is because a big flood once swept through the city and left its mark on the monument. Actually, it's just because the people who built it had to switch to a different type of stone. The new stone changed color over time.

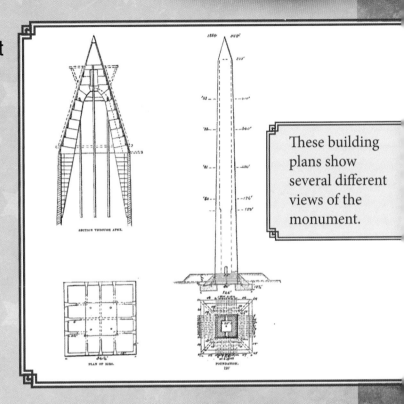

These building plans show several different views of the monument.

## EXPLORE MORE!

THE WASHINGTON MONUMENT WAS THE TALLEST BUILDING IN THE WORLD WHEN IT WAS BUILT. IT STOOD JUST OVER 555 FEET (169 M) TALL WHEN IT WAS FINISHED IN 1884. THE MONUMENT HELD THE WORLD RECORD UNTIL 1889, WHEN THE EIFFEL TOWER IN PARIS WAS COMPLETED.

# STANDING TALL FOR LIBERTY

The Statue of Liberty in New York Harbor was a gift from France to the United States. Even though it was a gift, the United States still had to pay for the **pedestal** on which the statue would stand. One popular story says that schoolchildren saved their pennies to pay for the statue's pedestal.

This story is only partly true. Many people, including children, sent in small amounts of money to help pay for the statue. But most of it was paid for by wealthy Americans.

## EXPLORE MORE!

CONSTRUCTION OF THE STATUE OF LIBERTY BEGAN IN FRANCE IN 1875. IT TOOK ABOUT NINE YEARS TO COMPLETE. THEN, IT HAD TO BE TAKEN APART AND SHIPPED TO THE UNITED STATES. IT WAS PUT TOGETHER AGAIN AND OPENED TO THE PUBLIC IN 1886.

The Statue of Liberty has been a symbol of freedom in America for more than 125 years.

# REPRESENTING HISTORY

Some U.S. symbols are all around us. U.S. flags fly at homes and schools. The Great Seal with the bald eagle appears on the dollar bill. We see them every day, but we might not think about what these important symbols represent.

The story behind each U.S. symbol is a part of American history. The country was formed based on ideals such as freedom, strength, and independence. Learning the true stories behind the symbols helps us understand how America became the nation that it is today.

## EXPLORE MORE!

HAVE YOU EVER WONDERED WHY AMERICA'S COLORS ARE RED, WHITE, AND BLUE? THE COUNTRY'S LEADERS CHOSE EACH COLOR FOR A SPECIAL REASON. RED STANDS FOR BRAVERY. WHITE REPRESENTS PEACE. FINALLY, BLUE STANDS FOR JUSTICE AND NOT GIVING UP.

A new star is added to the U.S. flag with each new state. The 50th star was added in 1960, about a year after Hawaii became a state.

# GLOSSARY

**Declaration of Independence:** The piece of writing in which the colonies said they were free from British rule.

**design:** The pattern or shape of something.

**document:** A formal piece of writing.

**federal:** Having to do with the national government.

**historian:** A person who studies history.

**image:** A picture made by an artist or camera.

**myth:** An idea or story that is believed by many people but that is not true.

**pedestal:** The base of a column or other tall object.

**proof:** Something that shows that something else is true or correct.

**recruitment:** The act of finding suitable people and getting them to join a group.

**represent:** To stand for.

**symbol:** A picture, shape, or object that stands for something else.

# FOR MORE INFORMATION

## BOOKS

Ferguson, Melissa. *American Symbols: What You Need to Know.* North Mankato, MN: Capstone Press, 2018.

Orr, Tamra B. *The Bald Eagle: All About the American Symbol.* North Mankato, MN: Pebble, 2021.

Schroeder, Alan. *Washington, DC from A to Z.* New York, NY: Holiday House, 2018.

## WEBSITES

**BrainPop: U.S. Symbols**
*jr.brainpop.com/socialstudies/citizenship/ussymbols/*
Check out this fun video to learn more about U.S. symbols.

**Ducksters: American Revolution: The United States Flag**
*www.ducksters.com/history/united_states_flag.php*
Find out more about how the flag got its start and how it has changed.

**National Geographic Kids: Statue of Liberty**
*kids.nationalgeographic.com/history/article/statue-of-liberty*
Learn more fun facts about Lady Liberty.

# INDEX